SUPERSCIENCE

FORCES AND MOTION

Rob Colson

W
FRANKLIN WATTS

This edition published in 2013 by
Franklin Watts
338 Euston Road
London NW1 3BH

Franklin Watts Australia
Level 17/207 Kent Street
Sydney NSW 2000

Produced for Franklin Watts by
Tall Tree Ltd

Editor: Jon Richards
Designer: Jonathan Vipond
Photographer: Ed Simkins
Consultant: Ade Deane-Pratt

A CIP catalogue record for this book is
available from the British Library.

Dewey Classification 531.1'1

ISBN 978 1 4451 2292 2

Printed in China

Franklin Watts is a division of Hachette
Children's Books, an Hachette UK company.

www.hachette.co.uk

Picture credits:
Front cover: main image Anthony Aneese Totah
Jr/Dreamstime.com, tr NASA, tc Amskad/
Dreamstime.com, tr Yuri Arcurs/Dreamstime.com,
1 TO COME, 3 Amskad/Dreamstime.com, 4 NASA,
5t Sally and Richard Greenhill/Alamy, 5b
Redeyed/Dreamstime.com, 6 Ekaterina
Petryakova/Dreamstime.com, 7l istockphoto, 7r
Amskad/Dreamstime.com, 8 Drazen Vukelic/
Dreamstime.com, 9t dan prat/istockphoto, 9b
wynnter/istockphoto, 10 Getty Images, 11t Patrick
Allen/Dreamstime.com, 12 Wojciechbeczynski/
Dreamstime.com, 13t Christian Lagereek.
Fahraeus/Dreamstime.com, 14 NickR/
Istockphoto, 15t NASA, 15bl Brad Calkins/
Dreamstime.com, 15br Feng Yu/Dreamstime.com,
16 Dreamstime.com, 17t Christophe Boisvieux/
Corbis, 17b Irochka/Dreamstime.com, 19t Shariff
Che' Lah/Dreamstime.com, 19b istockphoto, 20
Oleg Shelomentsev/Dreamstime.com, 21t NASA,
21b Diademimages/Dreamstime.com, 22t Andriy
Solovyov/Dreamstime.com, 23 Grondin Julien/
Dreamstime.com, 24 Kolbz/istockphoto, 25b Mitja
Mladkovic/Dreamstime.com, 26 David Lewis/
istockphoto, 27t Ken Hurst/Dreamstime.com, 28
Deborah Hewitt/Dreamstime.com, 29t Debra
James/Dreamstime.com, 29b Maxian/istockphoto

*Contents

*Why do things move?

Objects are moved by forces. Forces change the speed or direction of the object's motion or change its shape.

▌A universe in motion

Everything in the universe is on the move. In fact, if any of it stopped moving, it would cease to exist! At a scale too small for us to see, heat is caused by the vibration of tiny atoms. On a larger scale, the Earth orbits the Sun, while the solar system is just one small part of the Milky Way galaxy, which rotates around a central black hole. On the largest scale of all, the universe is expanding in all directions and everything is moving farther apart.

All the planets in the solar system orbit the Sun. The Sun is itself orbiting a distant black hole.

Neptune

Uranus

Saturn

Jupiter

Asteroid belt

Sun

Mercury

Venus

Earth

Moon

Mars

What are forces?

Forces are often described as pushes or pulls. They either change the speed or direction of an object or put it under pressure, changing its shape or breaking it. An object is always being affected by more than one force, and an object may be pushed, pulled, twisted and turned all at the same time. As you sit on a roundabout, force from the person pushing it around is making you spin, while the force of friction is slowing you down, and the force of gravity keeps you in your seat.

The force of pushing makes a roundabout go round. As more people climb on, you need to push all the harder.

When the train moves without moving

As the train on the left pulls away, passengers in the train on the right may feel that they are moving backwards.

The motion of one object is always measured relative to another object, which is called the frame of reference. In our everyday lives, we usually take the Earth as our frame of reference, but sometimes we can be fooled. If you sit in a stationary train and look over at the train next to you as it pulls away from the platform, you will feel like you are moving backwards. This is because your frame of reference has become the moving train rather than the Earth. Relative to the train going forwards, you are indeed going backwards.

*Action and reaction

When you sit, your weight presses down on the chair. But the chair also presses back up at you with the same force. Every time one object pushes another object, an equal force pushes back.

Equal and opposite forces

Forces always work in pairs, called the action and the reaction. The reaction is a force that is equal in size to the action but works in the opposite direction. To see how forces work in pairs, you can try a simple experiment. Stand facing a friend on rollerblades, and hold hands. Push against each other gently. You will find that you both move backwards. The force you make by pushing is the action, while the force of the other person pushing back is the reaction. The reaction is the force that moves you backwards.

If the two skaters push gently against each other, the force of reaction will move both of them backwards.

Newton's laws

An engraving of Newton made in 1856.

The English scientist Sir Isaac Newton (1643–1727) worked out the three basic laws of motion in the 17th century. Newton described for the first time how the motion of all things follows the same rules, from the movement of planets and stars right down to an apple falling from a tree. In the past century, it has been found that Newton's laws do not work at the scale of tiny atoms, but they do work for all the objects that we can see with the naked eye. Newton's Third Law of Motion describes action and reaction. It states that: 'For every action, there is an equal and opposite reaction.'

How do rockets move in space?

When a rocket takes off, it is propelled upwards by the force of its hot gases, which push against the air. In space, there is no air to press against, but the rocket is still powered forward by action and reaction. As the rocket forces the gases backwards out of its engine, the reaction of the gases pushes the rocket forward. A rocket needs a lot of force to take off and escape the Earth's gravity, but much less force when in space. Once in space, the Space Shuttle can zoom along at over 30,000 km/h.

Rockets need a lot of energy to take off and overcome the force of gravity pulling them back towards the Earth.

*Speeding up and slowing down

If there are no forces acting on it, an object will continue at the same speed in the same direction. Objects only speed up, slow down or change direction when a force acts on them.

The force of gravity pulling down and the force of air resistance pushing up against the parachute are equal, so the parachutist falls at a constant velocity.

Velocity

Velocity is an object's speed in a particular direction. Newton's First Law of Motion states that a net force is needed to change an object's velocity. 'Net' means the force that remains when all the forces acting on the object are added together. For instance, when an object is falling, the force of gravity speeds it up and the force of air resistance slows it down. The faster an object falls, the greater its air resistance. The falling object's velocity will continue to increase until the opposing forces of gravity and air resistance become equal.

Acceleration

A change in an object's velocity is called acceleration. If the net force is pushing in the same direction as the velocity, the object will speed up, or accelerate. If the net force is pushing against the direction of its velocity, the object will slow down, or decelerate. In a form of racing known as drag racing, cars accelerate as fast as they can along a 400-metre course. The cars are fitted with parachutes, which open up after the cars pass the finishing line to increase their air resistance and slow them down.

The fastest drag cars accelerate from 0 to over 500 km/h in less than five seconds.

Inertia

The 17th-century Italian astronomer Galileo Galilei (1564–1642) was the first person to understand correctly that an object will move with a constant velocity when no forces act on it, and will move with a constant acceleration when a constant force acts on it. This is called the Principle of Inertia. The greater an object's mass, the greater its inertia, which means that more force is needed to change its velocity by a given amount. Before Galileo, it was widely believed that a constant force was needed to keep an object moving.

Galileo has been described as the Father of Modern Science for his discoveries in physics.

*Momentum

The greater an object's inertia, the harder it is to start it moving, but also the harder it is to stop it once it is moving. The combination of a moving object's inertia and velocity is called its momentum.

When ski-jumpers land, they have lots of momentum and need plenty of space in which to slow down safely. Heavier skiers will need more space than lighter ones.

Overcoming momentum

Cars overcome their momentum to slow down by applying force on the wheels with the brakes. Skiers slow down by turning their skis sideways so that they dig into the snow. The heavier an object, the greater its momentum once it has started moving. An object that weighs 2 kilogrammes has twice the momentum of an object that weighs 1 kilogramme travelling at the same velocity, and it will take twice the force to slow it down.

The faster you go, the harder it is to stop

Mathematically, momentum increases by the square of the speed. This means that if you double an object's speed, you increase its momentum by 2 squared, or four times. A car travelling at 40 km/h has four times the momentum of a car travelling at 20 km/h, so when it brakes it will need four times the distance to slow down to a stop. In built-up areas with lots of pedestrians, it is important for safety that cars should have short braking distances, so strict speed limits are imposed.

Heavy cars such as SUVs have more momentum than light cars, so their braking distances are longer.

Project **Transferring momentum**

Marble (c) rolls off with the momentum gained from marble (a).

Marbles (a) and (b) are now motionless.

Here, the momentum from marble (a) has passed through marble (b) onto marble (c).

Momentum can pass from one object to another. To see this in action, you'll need three marbles of equal size and two rulers. Tape the rulers to a tabletop about 1 centimetre apart to form your track. Place two marbles in the track a few centimetres apart. Flick one marble onto the other. The first marble will stop moving when it hits the second marble, which will roll off. The momentum of the first marble has been transferred into the second one. Now place two marbles in the centre of the track touching each other and flick the third marble onto one of them. This time the momentum is passed from the moving marble onto the second touching marble through the first touching marble, which stays where it is.

*Friction

Friction is a force that causes moving objects to slow down. It is caused when one object rubs against another. The rougher the surfaces, the greater the friction caused by rubbing.

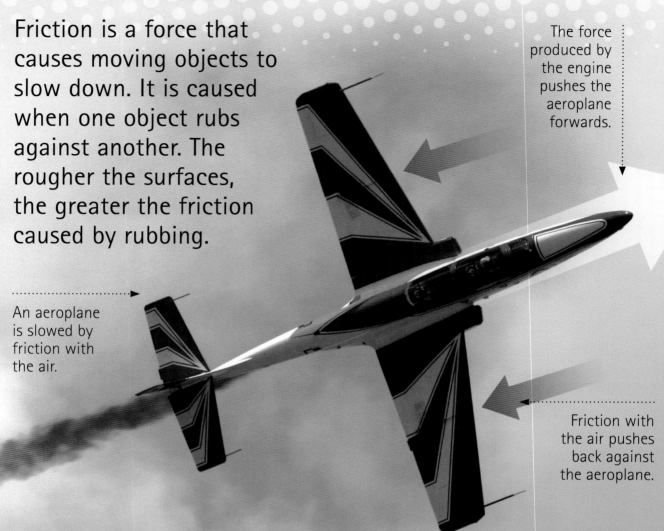

The force produced by the engine pushes the aeroplane forwards.

An aeroplane is slowed by friction with the air.

Friction with the air pushes back against the aeroplane.

Air resistance

As a car moves along a flat road, it needs to keep applying force to the wheels with its engine just to keep going at the same speed. This is because its forward movement is being opposed by the force of friction. The wheels rub against the road, causing rolling friction (see the project opposite). The car also rubs against the air as it moves through it, causing a kind of friction called air resistance. Vehicles minimise air resistance by having an aerodynamic shape, which means that they cut a smooth path through the air as they move.

Overcoming friction

As objects are slowed down by friction, they lose energy. The energy is mostly given off in the form of heat. You can feel this if you rub your hands together very fast. In just a few seconds, your hands will get hot. To keep machines running efficiently and stop them from overheating, friction between their moving parts needs to be kept to a minimum. This is done by making the surfaces as smooth as possible with oil or by using ball bearings, which roll between the surfaces.

Ball bearings sit between two moving surfaces and roll as they move, reducing rubbing and keeping friction to a minimum.

Project Slide or roll?

A soft ball resists movement by changing shape, or deforming, as it rolls, which is why flat tyres roll less well than pumped-up ones. This resistance is called rolling friction. A hard ball deforms very little as it rolls, so it produces very little rolling friction. A hard ball moves much more easily than a sliding object. To see this, slide a book along a hard floor. Now place six or seven marbles under the book and slide it again. The marbles stop the book from rubbing against the floor, and produce very little rolling friction, so the book slides much more easily.

The book slides very easily on the rolling marbles.

*Gravity

Gravity is a force that pulls objects together. All objects have a gravitational pull, but only large ones, such as the Earth, have a pull that is big enough to measure.

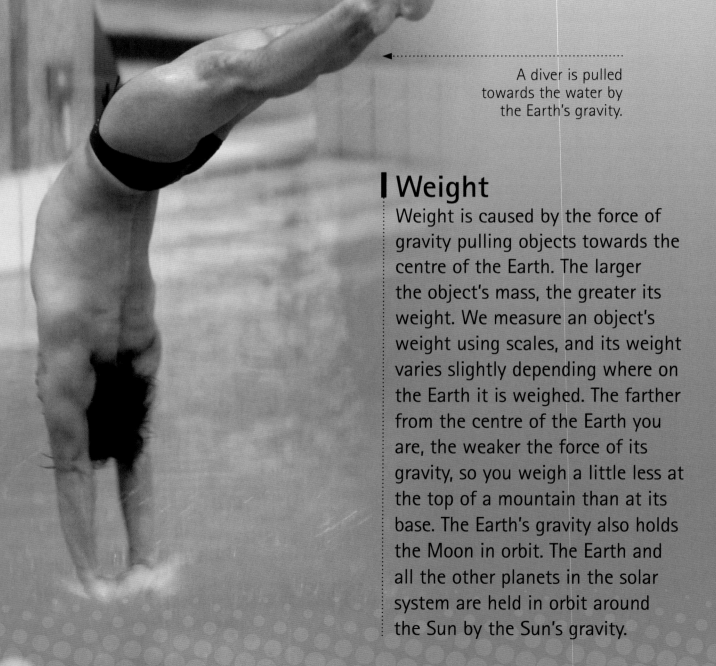

A diver is pulled towards the water by the Earth's gravity.

Weight

Weight is caused by the force of gravity pulling objects towards the centre of the Earth. The larger the object's mass, the greater its weight. We measure an object's weight using scales, and its weight varies slightly depending where on the Earth it is weighed. The farther from the centre of the Earth you are, the weaker the force of its gravity, so you weigh a little less at the top of a mountain than at its base. The Earth's gravity also holds the Moon in orbit. The Earth and all the other planets in the solar system are held in orbit around the Sun by the Sun's gravity.

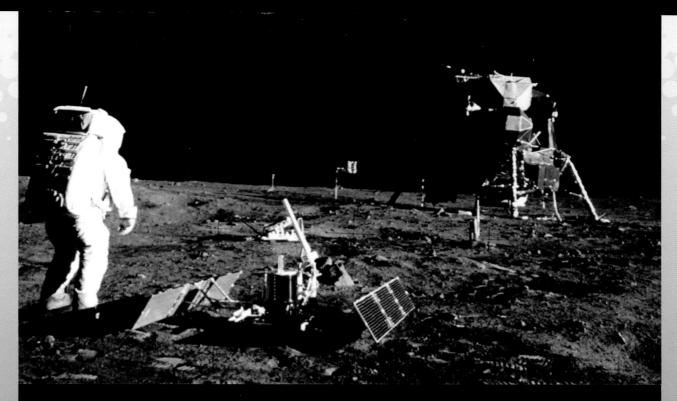

Astronauts walking on the Moon weighed just one sixth of their weight on Earth. Even wearing bulky spacesuits, they had no difficulty moving around.

Walking on the Moon

The size of an object's gravitational pull is directly proportional to its mass. The larger an object is, the greater its gravity. The gravitational pull on the surface of the Moon is just one sixth as strong as the pull on the surface of the much larger Earth. As they were so much lighter, the astronauts who walked on the Moon were able to jump much farther than they could on the Earth. Astronaut Alan Shepard hit three golf balls on the Moon, sending one ball over 200 metres with a one-armed swing of a six-iron club!

The hammer and feather test

All objects are accelerated towards the centre of the Earth by gravity at the same rate. Some objects, such as feathers, fall much more slowly than others because air resistance slows them down. The Moon does not have an atmosphere, so there is no air resistance on the Moon. During a moonwalk on the Apollo 15 space mission, astronaut David Scott dropped a hammer and a feather at the same time to show that they did indeed fall towards the Moon at the same rate.

✳Magnetism

Magnetism is a force that certain objects, called magnets, exert on other objects. The area around a magnet in which it exerts this force is called its magnetic field.

Iron filings spread out around a magnet to show the shape of its magnetic field.

| Opposites attract

All magnets have two poles, called north and south. Opposite poles attract, pulling towards each other. Like poles repel, pushing each other away. Try this with two magnets. Hold north to north and south to south, and they push each other away. Hold north to south and they pull onto each other. Some magnets are permanent magnets, which means that they are always magnetic. Temporary magnets are made by passing an electrical current through a material called a conductor. Every electrical current creates a magnetic field around it.

Magnetic substances

All substances are pulled by magnets, but some are much more strongly pulled than others. Substances that are strongly pulled by magnets, such as iron and steel, are called magnetic substances. Mine detectors use a magnet to detect steel mines hidden under the soil. Powerful temporary magnets are used to pick up heavy blocks of crushed steel-plated cans in recycling centres. To drop the block of cans, the electrical current is broken and the block instantly falls to the ground.

The powerful magnet in a mine detector sets off a magnetic field in the metallic mines. A sensor in the detector then picks up the mine's magnetism.

The magnetic Earth

Whichever way you turn a compass, its magnetic needle will point north.

The Earth is a giant magnet. Compasses use the Earth's magnetic field to show us which direction is north. The needle in the compass is a magnet made of steel. The needle is pivoted so that it can turn freely and align itself with the Earth's magnetism. Opposite poles attract each other, so the north pole of the needle points to the Earth's south pole. In fact, magnetically, the North Pole is actually a south pole! Some animals can sense the Earth's magnetism. Birds that migrate long distances each year use their sense of magnetism to tell them which way they are going.

*Turning forces

If an object is fixed at one point and a force is applied to it, the object will turn around the fixed point. This turning force is called a turning moment, and it is used in simple mechanisms called levers.

Opening and closing doors

The point at which a turning object pivots is called the fulcrum. The farther away from the fulcrum you apply a force, the more easily you can turn the object, but the farther you have to move to turn it. A door's fulcrum is hinged to make it easier to open and close. Try pushing an open door shut near the hinge. You don't have to push it very far, but you do have to push with a lot of force. Now push it shut from farther away from the hinge. It moves much more easily, but you have to move it much farther.

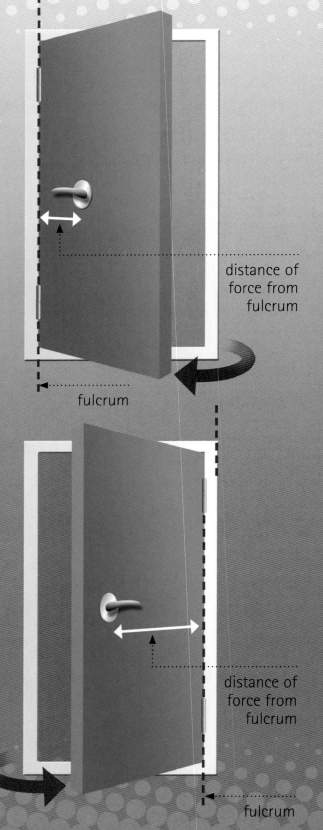

distance of force from fulcrum

fulcrum

distance of force from fulcrum

fulcrum

Opening the door from near the fulcrum (top) needs a greater force than opening it from farther away (bottom).

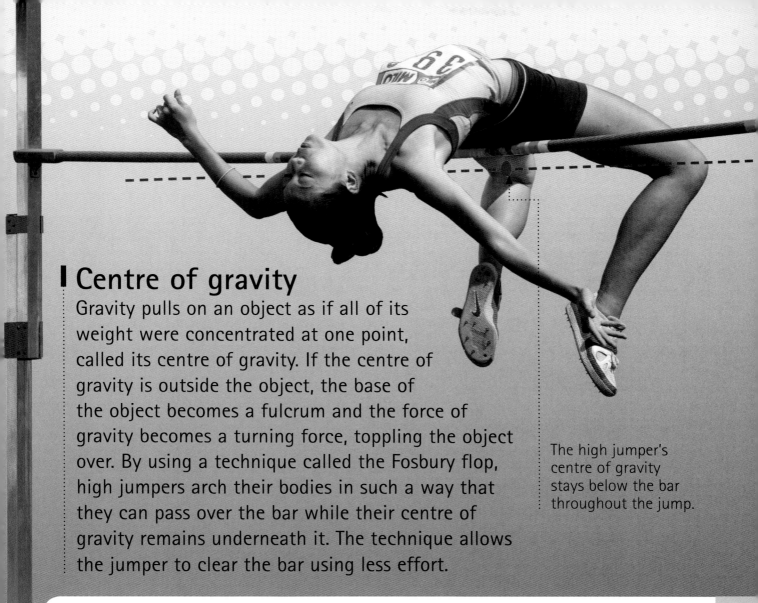

Centre of gravity

Gravity pulls on an object as if all of its weight were concentrated at one point, called its centre of gravity. If the centre of gravity is outside the object, the base of the object becomes a fulcrum and the force of gravity becomes a turning force, toppling the object over. By using a technique called the Fosbury flop, high jumpers arch their bodies in such a way that they can pass over the bar while their centre of gravity remains underneath it. The technique allows the jumper to clear the bar using less effort.

The high jumper's centre of gravity stays below the bar throughout the jump.

Project Levers

Levers use turning moments to change the amount of effort needed to move objects. Our arms are levers with fulcrums at the shoulder and elbow. The farther from the fulcrums you hold a load, the more effort it takes to keep it there. Try this by holding your upper arm by your side and bending your elbow so that your lower arm is parallel to the floor in front of you. Hold a fairly heavy bag in your hand and feel its weight. Now extend your arm out straight from the shoulder. The bag now feels much heavier as the fulcrum is at the shoulder, roughly twice as far away.

These athletes are lifting weights using their elbows as the fulcrum.

*Moving in circles

An object that is moving in circles is constantly changing direction. Two forces are acting on it, one moving it forwards, the other pulling it inwards and changing its direction.

Angular momentum

A spinning top will stay upright as long as it is spinning fast enough. A spinning object has angular momentum, which means that it resists any force trying to change its direction. As long as the top spins around its centre of gravity, the force of gravity will not affect its angular momentum, so it stays upright. In much the same way, you cannot close a door by pushing it at the hinges. Over time, friction slows the top down and its spinning becomes irregular. Now gravity can affect its momentum and it eventually falls over.

The top's angular momentum stops gravity from toppling it over.

Orbiting the Earth

The Moon is held in Earth's orbit by gravity.

The Moon orbits the Earth once every 27.3 days. It travels at an almost constant speed in its orbit, moving at about 3,700 km/h relative to the Earth. The Moon is, however, constantly accelerating. This is because the force of the Earth's gravity is pulling it inwards, providing the centripetal force that constantly changes the Moon's direction and keeps it in its orbit. If the Earth's gravity were removed, the Moon would fly off into space in a straight line.

▎Centripetal force

The force that pulls a spinning object from the centre of its spin and constantly changes its direction is called centripetal force. Stand in an open space well away from any furniture, hold your arms out wide and spin round a few times. Don't go too fast or you'll make yourself dizzy. The faster you spin, the larger your angular momentum and the greater the centripetal force pulling your arms in. You will feel your muscles at the shoulder working to provide the centripetal force.

A spinning figure skater can speed up her spin by pulling her arms in. This reduces the centripetal force in the spin. Her angular momentum stays the same, so she spins more quickly to compensate for the reduction in centripetal force.

*Pressure

A force applies pressure to the objects it acts on. The smaller the area a force is concentrated on, the greater the pressure that area experiences. Too much pressure and the object may break.

Concentrating pressure

If you try to slice a loaf of bread with the flat side of the knife, you won't get very far. You need to concentrate all the pressure you are putting on the bread on the narrow, sharp edge of the knife. Drawing pins work in the same way. The pressure from the finger forcing the pin into a noticeboard is spread out over the wide end of the pin so that you don't hurt your finger. At the other end, all that pressure is concentrated in one sharp point, and the pin is forced into the board.

The sharp point of a drawing pin can apply enough pressure to pierce a noticeboard.

Project Water pressure

The deeper under water you go, the greater the weight of the water above you pushing down. This increased pressure can make your ears hurt when you dive to the bottom of a deep swimming pool. To see the effect of depth on pressure, pierce a row of four holes down the side of a large plastic bottle. Plug the holes on the outside with modelling clay and fill the bottle with water. Remove the plugs and watch how the water is forced out of the holes. The nearer the bottom of the bottle, the farther the jets of water travel under the increasing pressure.

As the pressure increases with depth, the lower jet of water is sent farther.

Taking the strain

When you push against a fixed solid object, it pushes back at you with an equal force, but you are also placing that object under stress. If you push with sufficient pressure, the stress will reach the object's breaking point, and it breaks. Volcanoes erupt through weak points in Earth's crust. The hot magma (liquid rock) under the surface exerts pressure on the weak point. The pressure builds up over years and centuries until it reaches the breaking point of the crust, and the magma explodes through to the surface.

Large eruptions can occur after a long period in which the pressure under the surface has had time to build up.

*Stretching and squashing

A force can move or break solid objects. It also changes their shape, stretching or squashing them around the area the pressure is applied.

Elasticity and plasticity

Some material, such as modelling clay, changes shape when force is applied to it and stays in the new shape when the force is removed. This is called a plastic substance. Elastic material, such as rubber, snaps back to its original shape when the force that is squashing or stretching it is removed. If you squash or stretch rubber many times, it eventually loses its elasticity and only partially returns to the original shape or returns to that shape more slowly. Old tennis balls lose elasticity, meaning that they do not spring off a racquet as well as new balls.

A tennis ball squashes when it is hit by a racquet, then springs back into shape to speed it back over the net.

Project Spring balances

The distance a spring stretches, or extends, is directly proportional to the force that is applied to it. Double the force and the extension doubles. Spring balances work by measuring the extension of a spring, which tells you how heavy the weight is. Try this by hanging a spring from a hook. Measure the length of the spring with no weight. Now hang a weight such as a metal ring from the spring and measure its length. Subtract the original length to see how much it has extended. Try two and then four weights. The extension doubles each time you double the weight.

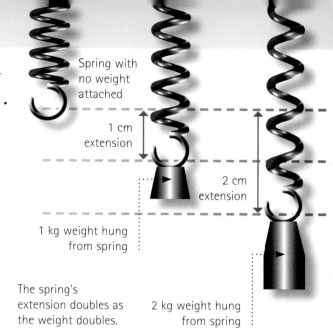

Spring with no weight attached

1 cm extension

2 cm extension

1 kg weight hung from spring

The spring's extension doubles as the weight doubles.

2 kg weight hung from spring

By pulling the bow back, an archer is giving the bow potential energy, which is released to fire the arrow forwards.

Using elasticity

When you stretch or squash an elastic material, force is transferred into the material, which is now said to contain potential energy. The material uses its potential energy to return to its original shape when the pressure is released. An archer uses the potential energy in the stretched string of the bow to fire an arrow. If you wrap a group of pencils together with an elastic band, you have to keep wrapping the band around the pencils until it stretches. Only a stretched elastic band has the energy to hold the pencils together.

*Using forces to move our bodies

The bones in our bodies are connected to each other at joints. The joints act as fulcrums. The bones are moved around the joints by muscles that apply turning forces.

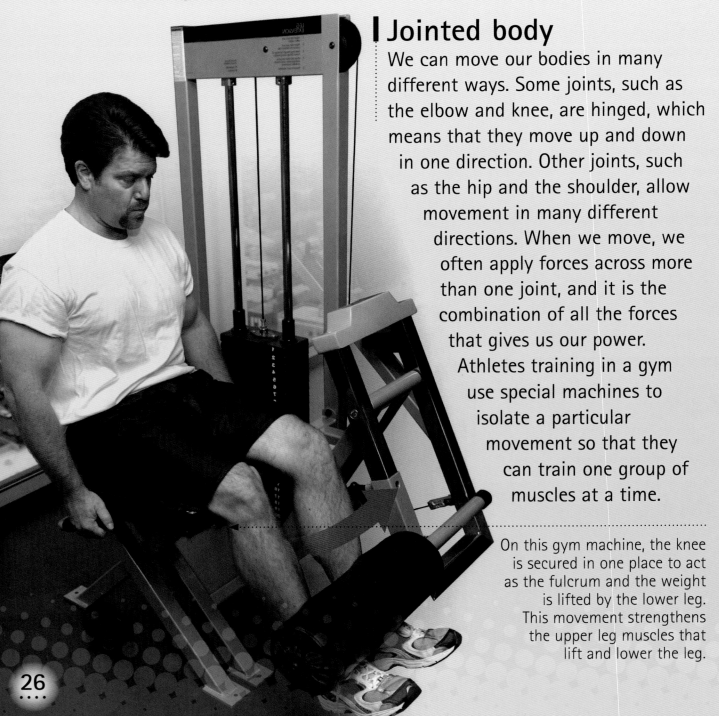

Jointed body

We can move our bodies in many different ways. Some joints, such as the elbow and knee, are hinged, which means that they move up and down in one direction. Other joints, such as the hip and the shoulder, allow movement in many different directions. When we move, we often apply forces across more than one joint, and it is the combination of all the forces that gives us our power. Athletes training in a gym use special machines to isolate a particular movement so that they can train one group of muscles at a time.

On this gym machine, the knee is secured in one place to act as the fulcrum and the weight is lifted by the lower leg. This movement strengthens the upper leg muscles that lift and lower the leg.

Lifting correctly

We can minimise the effort we use when lifting by using our bodies correctly. If you lift a heavy box by bending over from the hip, you are increasing the distance of the weight from the fulcrum at the hip, which means that you have to use more force, or turning moment, to lift the box. If you squat down to lift the box, you keep the turning moment to a minimum, which makes it easier to lift. By squatting, you are also able to use your powerful thigh muscles to do most of the work.

Always bend your knees when you lift heavy objects and try to keep your back as straight as possible.

Muscle power

Muscles can only apply a pulling force. They cannot push. To move a joint in two directions, muscles are grouped in pairs. To straighten the bones at a joint, a muscle called an extensor contracts to pull on the bone. To bend bones at the joint, the extensor relaxes and a muscle called a flexor contracts to pull in the opposite direction. You have lots of pairs of extensors and flexors in your body, including pairs to move the elbow, wrist, knee and heel. Bend and straighten each of these joints in turn and feel which muscle contracts with the movement.

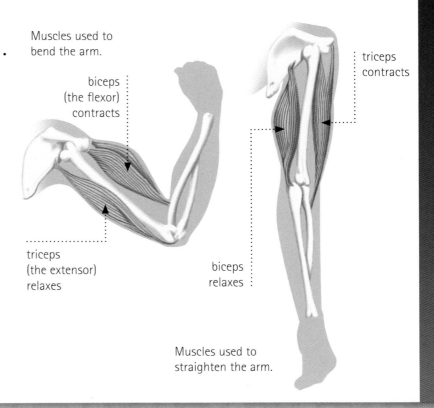

Muscles used to bend the arm.

biceps (the flexor) contracts

triceps (the extensor) relaxes

triceps contracts

biceps relaxes

Muscles used to straighten the arm.

*Using forces to do our work

As well as using forces to move our bodies, people have come up with lots of clever machines that use forces to help us do our work more easily.

❙ Water power

Flowing water has been used for thousands of years to help us do work such as grinding flour. The water pushes on the blades of a large wheel, changing the forward motion of the river into the circular motion of the wheel. The wheel turns an axle that drives the mill's machinery. The circular motion of the axle may be turned back into forward motion using a system of cogs called a rack and pinion. Watermills used to be a common sight by the side of rivers, but have now been replaced by motors in most parts of the world.

The large wheel is turned by the flowing water.

Lifting machines

Cranes are machines that lift heavy objects. They work by pulling on the load, which is connected to a wire wrapped around a winder. As the winder is turned by the crane's engine, it winds the wire up, shortening its length and changing the circular winding force into a linear (straight line) pulling force, which raises the weight. The wire is run over a pulley, which changes the direction of the pull. The winders in modern cranes are powered by large engines. In the past, horses walking in circles were used to power the winder.

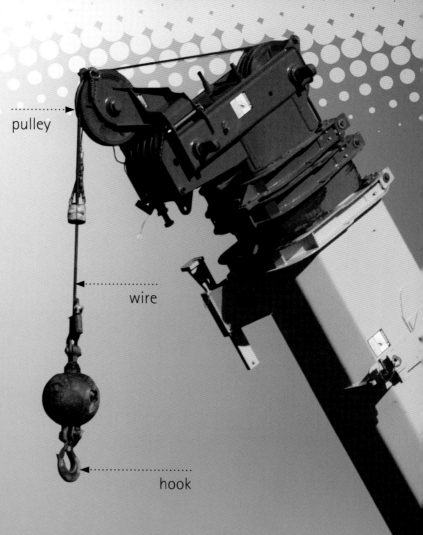

pulley

wire

hook

Project Forces in action

Which forces do you apply when you ride a bicycle?

When you ride a bicycle, many different forces are being applied to move you forwards. List all the forces that you can think of. Which forces drive the circular motion of the pedals and the wheels? How is the force transferred from one part of the bicycle to another? Where are the fulcrums for turning motion? What difference does it make to the force you need to apply when you pull on different places on the handlebars? Which muscles and joints are you using to turn the pedals? Which forces are resisting your movement? What kind of force do the brakes apply to slow you down?

*Glossary

Ball bearing
A small metal ball placed between surfaces to reduce friction.

Braking distance
The distance a vehicle travels from the moment the brakes are applied until it reaches a complete stop.

Elastic
Able to return to the original shape after being stretched or squashed.

Electrical current
The movement of tiny particles called electrons through a substance, which generates electricity.

Energy
A property of matter, which measures its ability to exert a force.

Extension
The distance by which an object such as a spring has been stretched.

Field
The area around an object in which a particular force exerted by that object, such as magnetism or gravity, can act.

Mass
The amount of matter contained in an object.

Orbit
The path taken by one celestial body around another. The Moon orbits the Earth, while the Earth orbits the Sun.

Plastic
A property of some matter, which means that it stays in its new shape after it has been stretched or squashed.

Potential energy
The energy contained in an object due to its position or state.

Pressure
A measure of a continuous force applied to an object.

Propel
To push forwards.

Transfer
To move from one object to another.

Weight
The force caused by the action of gravity on an object's mass.

*Resources

Essential Science: Forces and Friction, by Peter Riley (Franklin Watts, 2006) A guide to topics covered in the national curriculum, fully illustrated and with lots of fun activities.

The Real Scientist: Heave!, by Peter Riley (Franklin Watts, 2008) Ideas for investigations and experiments, plus explanations of scientific theories.

The Way Things Work, by David Macauley (DK, 2004) An illustrated guide to the science behind machines we use in everyday life.

Do Try This At Home!, by Punk Science (Children's Books, 2008) Experiment ideas for 'punk scientists', with a DVD of the experiments.

Richard Hammond's Blast Lab, by Richard Hammond (DK, 2009) The TV presenter shows how to do the experiments he carried out on his science show *Blast Lab*.

The Horrible Science of Everything, by Nick Arnold and Tony De Saulles (Scholastic, 2008) An exploration of the yucky side of science.

Websites

www.bbc.co.uk/schools/ks2bitesize
Games, quizzes and fun revision notes on a wide range of science topics.

www.sciencemuseum.org.uk
The website of London's Science Museum, with features on the history of science and the latest scientific discoveries.

www.practicalphysics.org/go/Topic_3
Experiments that explain all the basic concepts of physics, with notes for teachers.

www.sciencewithme.com
Games and science project ideas, with worksheets and colouring books to print out. A subscription website that's free to join.

www.scienceprojectideas.co.uk
Facts, figures and trivia about forces and motion and other areas of science, plus articles giving advice and help for parents and teachers.

*Index